Ferries

by Lola M. Schaefer

Consultant:
Pat McCarthy
Lake Michigan Carferry
Ludington, Michigan

Bridgestone Books
an imprint of Capstone Press
Mankato, Minnesota

Bridgestone Books are published by Capstone Press
818 North Willow Street, Mankato, Minnesota 56001
http://www.capstone-press.com

Library of Congress Cataloging-in-Publication Data
Schaefer, Lola M., 1950–
    Ferries/by Lola M. Schaefer.
    p. cm.—(The transportation library)
    Includes bibliographical references and index.
    Summary: Discusses the history and uses of ferries, the different kinds, and how
they work.
    ISBN 0-7368-0362-9
    1. Ferries—Juvenile literature. [1. Ferries.] I. Title. II. Series.
VM421.S33 2000
386'.6—dc21   99-14449
                                                                                      CIP

Editorial Credits

Karen L. Daas and Blanche R. Bolland, editors; Timothy Halldin, cover designer and
    illustrator; Heather Kindseth, illustrator; Kimberly Danger, photo researcher

Photo Credits

Bruce Coleman Inc./Steve Bloom, 18–19
James P. Rowan, 20
Photri-Microstock, 10–11, 14–15, 16–17
Shaffer Photography/James L. Shaffer, 6
Unicorn Stock Photos, cover; Unicorn Stock Photos/Ronald E. Partis, 8
Visuals Unlimited/Mark E. Gibson, 4; William J. Weberg, 10 (inset)

Table of Contents

Ferries

Ferries are boats that carry passengers across water. People take ferries where no bridge crosses a body of water. Some ferries also carry cars and other vehicles. People can drive their cars onto these ferries.

vehicle
something that carries people and goods from one place to another

Traveling by Ferry

A ferry picks up passengers at a dock. People buy tickets at the dock. They then walk up a gangway onto the ferry. This walkway joins the ferry to the dock. Some passengers drive vehicles up a gangway to the ferry.

passenger
someone other than the captain who travels on a ferry or other vehicle

Ferry Crossings

A ferry leaves the dock at a set time. The captain then steers the ferry away from the dock. Some ferry crossings are short. Other crossings can take many hours.

captain's bridge

captain's bridge

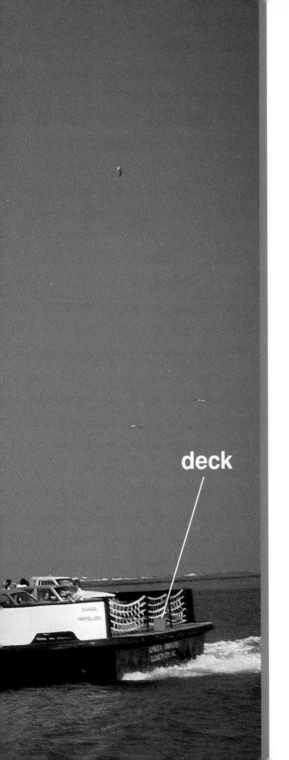

deck

Parts of a Ferry

Most ferries have the same main parts. The captain steers the ferry from the captain's bridge. Passengers sit or stand on the deck. Vehicles also are on the deck. Some ferries have more than one deck.

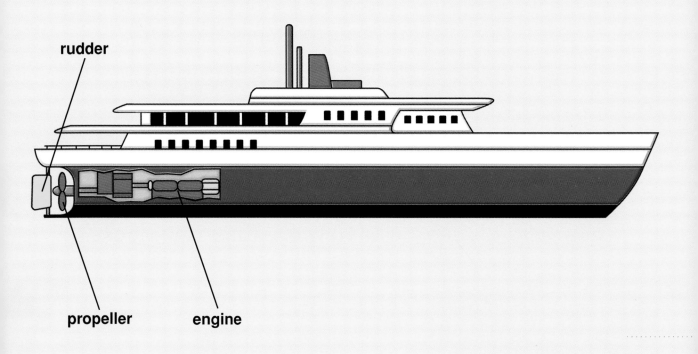

rudder

propeller   engine

How a Ferry Works

Ferries work like many other boats. A ferry's engines turn propellers. Propellers push water to move the ferry forward. The captain uses a steering wheel to move the rudders. Rudders turn the ferry.

rudder
a plate at the back of a boat; a captain uses a rudder to steer the ferry

Before the Ferry

People have traveled on water for thousands of years. American Indians used canoes to take explorers and traders across rivers. Later, flat-bottom boats carried settlers, wagons, and horses across water.

Early Ferries

People used long oars or poles to push early ferries across water. Later, people stretched rope or wire across a river. They joined these lines to ferries. The river current then pushed the ferries along the rope or wire. Around 1790, the first engine-powered ferry crossed a river.

current
the movement of water in a body of water such as a river or ocean

Ferries around the World

People all over the world travel by ferry. Ferries carry passengers and railroad cars between Japan's islands. Many ferries cross the English Channel between England and France.

Ferry Facts

- Ferries that make long trips have restaurants and sleeping rooms for passengers.

- The *Filja Europa* is the largest ferry in the world. It can carry 3,000 passengers, 65 semi-trailer trucks, and 350 cars. It travels between Stockholm, Sweden, and Helsinki, Finland.

- Ferries cross the English Channel 130 times each day during the summer.

- Most ferries can load or unload at both ends.

Hands On: A Ferry's Load

Even heavy boats can float. You can learn how ferries can carry heavy vehicles and still float.

What You Need

Large bowl
Water
Modeling clay
Sand or 2 boxes of paperclips

What You Do

1. Fill the bowl half full of water.
2. Make a large ball with the clay.
3. Place the ball of clay in the water. The ball will sink.
4. Remove the clay from the water. Shape the clay into a boat with sides. Place it in the water. The boat will float.
5. Slowly put sand or paperclips in the boat. Stop filling your boat when water is near the top.

The ball of clay and the boat are the same weight. But the shape of the boat allows it to float. The boat pushes water out and away from it. The shape also spreads the boat's weight over a larger area. The ball sinks because it does not push enough water away.

Words to Know

engine (EN-juhn)—a machine that makes the power needed to move something

explorer (ek-SPLOR-ur)—a person who travels to new places

gangway (GANG-way)—a short bridge used for walking on and off a boat or ship

propeller (pruh-PEL-ur)—a set of turning blades that move a ferry through water

rudder (RUHD-ur)—a plate on the back of a boat; a captain uses a rudder to steer a ferry.

Read More

Flanagan, Alice K. *Riding the Ferry with Captain Cruz.* Our Neighborhood. New York: Children's Press, 1996.
Jeunesse, Gallimard. *Boats.* A First Discovery Book. New York: Scholastic, 1993.
Maynard, Christopher. *The Usborne Book of Cutaway Boats.* London: Usborne Publishing, 1996.

Internet Sites

The Historic Ferry *Yankee*: Museum
http://historicferryyankee.com/museum.htm
Lake Michigan Carferry: S.S. *Badger*
http://www.ssbadger.com
Washington State Ferries: Ferry Fleet Guide
http://www.wsdot.wa.gov/ferries/fleet-guide/fg-index.htm

Index